Words Are Not for Hurting

Elizabeth Verdick

Illustrated by Marieka Heinlen

free spirit
PUBLISHING®
Works for kids®

Library of Congress Cataloging-in-Publication Data

Verdick, Elizabeth.
   Words are not for hurting / Elizabeth Verdick ; illustrated by Marieka Heinlen.
      p. cm.
   Summary: Encourages toddlers and preschoolers to express themselves using helpful, not hurtful, words. Includes a note for parents and caregivers.
   ISBN 1-57542-156-9
1. Conversation—Juvenile literature. 2. Etiquette for children and teenagers. [1. Conversation. 2. Etiquette.] I. Heinlen, Marieka, ill. II. Title.
   BJ2121.V47 2004
   177'.2—dc22

                                                                                    2003021273

Cover and interior design by Marieka Heinlen

10 9 8 7 6 5 4 3 2
Printed in Hong Kong

Free Spirit Publishing Inc.
217 Fifth Avenue North, Suite 200
Minneapolis, MN 55401-1299
(612) 338-2068
help4kids@freespirit.com
www.freespirit.com

The following are registered trademarks of Free Spirit Publishing Inc.:

FREE SPIRIT®
FREE SPIRIT PUBLISHING®
THE FREE SPIRITED CLASSROOM®
SELF-HELP FOR KIDS®
SELF-HELP FOR TEENS®
WORKS FOR KIDS®
HOW RUDE!™
LEARNING TO GET ALONG™
LAUGH & LEARN™

free spirit
PUBLiSHiNG®
Works for kids®

Learning to Get Along™

Laugh & Learn®

For my children, Olivia and Zachary.
Every day, you teach me more
about love and patience,
and you always make me smile.
—E.V.

For my mother and father,
whose words of encouragement
helped me believe in myself.
—M.H.

Dear Parents and Caregivers,

Children are known for saying whatever comes to mind. Their words—so often funny, surprising, and insightful—are a window into their feelings.

I'll never forget when my own daughter, at age four, was eating her first ice-cream sundae and announced with excitement, "Every day should be hot-fudge sundae—even Saturday!" This little nugget of wisdom still makes me laugh. There are times, though, when we hear children saying something mean or hurtful. They might tease another child, for example, or make unkind comments about someone's appearance. They might shout, or even swear. What's behind these words? Often feelings of anger, sadness, rejection, confusion, or fear. Just like adults, children may lash out with a raised voice or hurtful words.

All of us—young and old alike—can learn to choose our words wisely. We can think before we speak and make an effort to use words that convey kindness and respect.

Most important, we can apologize when something we've said has hurt someone else. Those two little words, "I'm sorry," are sometimes so hard for us to say. But the more we practice, the better we get at it. And those two little words can make all the difference!

Elizabeth

P.S. On pages 28–32, you'll find activities, discussion starters, and other resources that reinforce the message of using helpful, not hurtful, words.

Did you know it takes only 26 letters
to make *millions* of words?

Nn Oo Pp Qq Rr Ss Tt Uu Vv Ww Xx Yy Zz

Some words are really *loooong:*

"Thingamajig"

"Mississippi"

"Abracadabra!"

And some are just plain silly:

"Wiggly Giggly"

"Cock-a-doodle-doo!"

Words help you say lots of
important things, like:

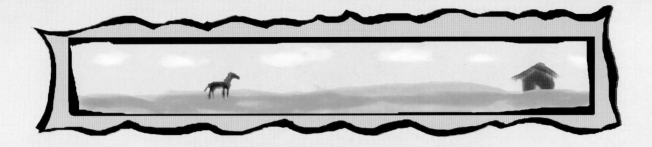

"You're welcome."

"Thank you for helping me."

DINO PUZZLE

5

Sometimes your words are LOUD!

"Ready or not,
here I come!"

And sometimes
your words
are soft.

"Shhhh..."

6

Sometimes your words are funny.

"Knock knock."   "Who's there?"

Sometimes you
even sing them.

"La la la la"

CHALK

Your words belong to you.
You choose what to say and how to say it.

Your words can hurt or your words can help.

These are helpful words:

"Let's work together."

"Do you want to share this with me?"

13

Words are not for hurting.
When you hear hurtful words,
how do you feel? Maybe...

Sad

Mad

Scared

15

When you say hurtful words, how do you feel?

16

Maybe you feel sorry and wish
you hadn't said them.

There's something you can do.
You can take them back. Like this:

"I shouldn't
have said
those things."

Here are two other words you can say:
"I'm sorry."

Those two little words
can be a BIG help.

21

When you hear hurtful words,
what can you do? You can say:

"Words are not for hurting.
Please don't say those things."

Or you can tell a grown-up:

"He's teasing me.
Can you help?"

23

Your words are important.
If you think before you speak,
you can use your words well.

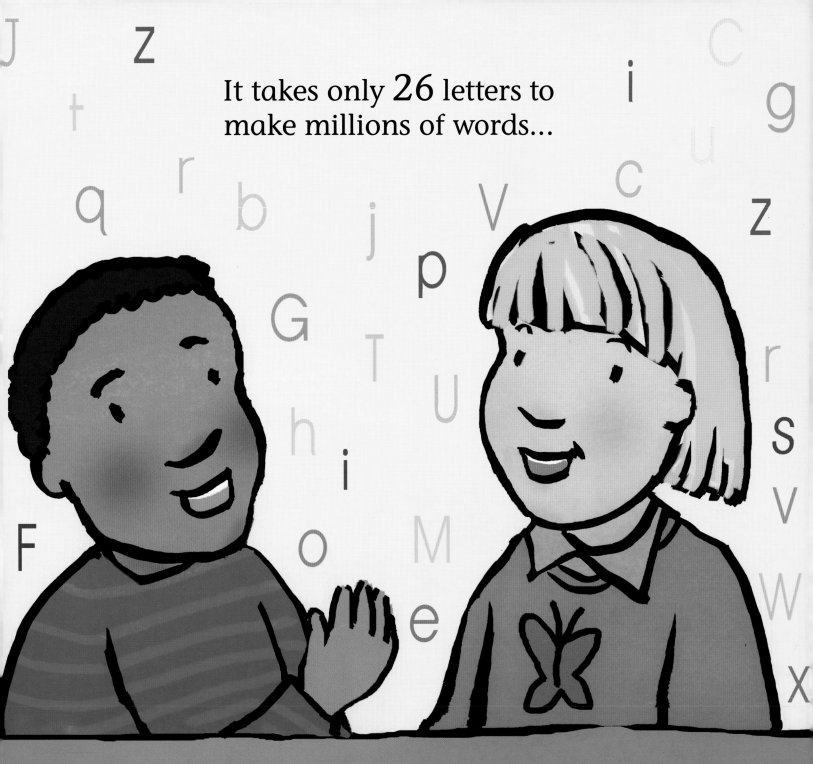

...so you've got lots of words to choose from!

You can tell this to yourself and to others:

"Words are not for hurting."

Activities and Discussion Starters

How We Use Words

Communication Explanation

Talk to children about what communication means. When we communicate, we use our words to say something to someone else. Every day we use words in so many ways, both spoken and written. Talk about how we use words to greet others, tell stories, sing songs, ask questions, and much more.

Fun with Words

Have children use words in creative ways. If some of the children speak a second language, ask them to teach a few new words to the other kids. Count to 10 (or higher) in another language. Or, talk about words that rhyme, words that are silly, or words that are very short or long. Have the children imagine a world without words—what would it be like if we couldn't communicate with each other verbally?

Signs and Symbols

Talk about ways we use special signs, symbols, and gestures to communicate. For example, there are signs for "hello" (a wave), "peace" (a peace sign formed with two fingers or written as a symbol), and "love" (blowing a kiss, or writing x's and o's).

American Sign Language (ASL) is the fourth most used language in the United States today. Talk with children about how this language of gestures and hand symbols can express words and concepts. Learn the gesture for "I love you" and practice it together. For a sign language resource, see page 32.

"Talking" Without Words

What Your Face Says

Help children understand that we "talk" with more than our mouth—our face also sends messages about what we are thinking or feeling. Invite children to make faces that match the feelings you introduce: happy, sad, mad, scared, or excited. Using a hand mirror, give each child a chance to look at himself or herself making an expressive face. Ask others in the group how the child is feeling, and how his or her face shows it. To connect this activity to *Words Are Not for Hurting*, discuss how facial expressions can be hurtful or helpful. Ask children how they would feel if someone scowled at them and said, "You can't play with us." Next, talk about ways they could help someone who's wearing a sad or scared expression. Try to notice whenever children are doing a good job of "reading others."

What Your Body Says

Introduce the idea of body language by explaining how our actions and gestures may do the talking for us. Demonstrate some body language yourself: lower your head to show that you're feeling sad or shy; stomp your foot to show anger; shrug your shoulders to suggest that you're unsure; take a step backward and hold your arms inward to show fear. Next, point out that "reading" someone's body language and facial expression can let you know how the person is feeling. If you wish, turn to pages 4–5 or 12–13 in *Words Are Not for Hurting*, which show children and adults using different body language. Ask what each person might be thinking or feeling. Invite volunteers to show how they might respond to these feelings in helpful ways.

What Your Mind Says

Ask children to think about how they talk to themselves inside their head. Is there a voice saying kind and positive things like, "You can do it" and "That was a good try"? Or is there a voice saying negative things like, "You always do things wrong"? Talk about how the words inside our own head can be hurtful or helpful. When we tell ourselves something positive ("I will try my hardest"), we feel stronger and we're more likely to succeed than if we tell ourselves, "I better not try since I might fail." Help each child think of one positive message to use throughout the day such as, "I can do it" or "I can give it a try."

Positive Ways to Use Words

"Feelings" Words

Children can learn to recognize their feelings and put their emotions into words. Once they have words for their own feelings, children are better able to recognize and respond to the feelings of others. Talk about words that describe how we feel: happy, sad, cranky, mad, worried, lonely, surprised, nervous, excited, sleepy, energetic, and so on. To reinforce the lessons in "What Your Face Says" and "What Your Body Says," act out some of the emotions using clear facial expressions and body language. Have the children act out telling someone else how they feel: "I am sad," "I feel so excited!" or "I am angry."

Polite Words

Good manners help children treat others with kindness and respect. Point out that "please" and "thank you" are among the most helpful words that people use. To help children understand the importance of polite words, give them examples of not using them: "Get off the swings!" vs. "May I please have a turn on the swings?" Talk about how it feels to do something nice for someone else but not hear the words "thank you" afterward. Or, ask children how it would feel if someone bumped into them hard but never said, "Excuse me" or "Sorry." Practice saying polite words; compliment children whenever you overhear them using good manners.

Tone of Voice

Many children already know the difference between "indoor" and "outdoor" voices, and have learned to use a quieter voice while inside. Yet, they may need help understanding the subtler lesson of how our tone of voice can make a difference in how others interpret and respond to our words. To give children an example of how this works, you might use a loud, demanding tone of voice and say, "It's MY turn to go first! You always go first and it's not FAIR!" Talk about how someone who hears words like these might feel. Next, say the words in a slightly different way and in a gentler tone of voice: "It's my turn to go first now. You went first last time, and it's only fair that I get a chance to, too." Ask the children how they feel when they hear the words spoken in this way. Explain that how we sound plays a big part in what we actually communicate to others.

Talk About It

You may want to discuss some of the concepts introduced in *Words Are Not for Hurting*: Your words belong to you and think before you speak. Ask children what they think these concepts mean. Talk about how our words come from our head and our heart; we use words to express how we think and feel, and this is why our words are ours.

Each one of us chooses what to say and how to say it. Yet, it isn't uncommon for children to try to blame someone else for something hurtful they've said. For example, you might hear an excuse like, "Andre told me to say it!" or "She said it first!" Talk about how each person must take responsibility for what he or she says. Discuss why shifting blame on someone else doesn't help.

Ask children if they're familiar with the phrase, "Hold your tongue" (it makes for a good visual). See if they can connect it to the idea of "Think before you speak." To help children put this idea into practice, suggest that the next time they're about to say something cruel or hurtful to somebody else they take a deep breath instead and count to 5 in their head. After thinking about it, can they come up with a better, kinder way to say what they feel? Or, can they decide to say nothing at all?

Words That Hurt

Stick and Stones

There's an old saying that children may be familiar with: "Sticks and stones may break my bones, but words will never hurt me." Ask them what they think this saying means, and whether they believe it's true. Can words hurt—why or why not? What are some examples of hurtful words (name-calling, teasing, etc.). Talk about how it feels to be teased, or yelled at, or called a rude name. To take this further, talk about how it feels to tease others—does this lead to positive feelings? Why not?

Sticking Up for Yourself

Talk about the importance of sticking up for yourself when someone says something hurtful—and for sticking up for others who are teased as well. Offer examples of ways to do this, such as: "Words are not for hurting," or "That hurts my feelings," or "Please stop saying things like that." Let children know that another option is to find a grown-up who can help. Ask them to name some adults they can go to for assistance—parents, grandparents or other relatives, teachers, childcare providers, baby-sitters, and so on.

A Word to Grown-ups

Young children are like sponges, soaking up everything around them. They listen to our words, even when we think they aren't listening. They may overhear grown-ups yelling, cursing, gossiping, criticizing, or using words in other hurtful ways. Children may then imitate what they hear. As adults, we can make an effort to choose words that are kind, loving, and peaceful. If we slip up, we can acknowledge it, apologize, and let children know that we'll try harder next time.

"Bad Words"

In your classroom or home, you probably have rules against using "bad words" (swearing, for example). Children may swear to express anger, to test their boundaries, or simply because they've heard the words from adults in their lives and don't yet realize the effect they have. Talk about how these particular words make others feel: upset, angry, embarrassed, uncomfortable. You can help children understand that using inappropriate words has consequences, such as a brief time-out.

Words That Help

Questions

Children need to know that asking a question is a great way to find out more—whether they're confused about something or simply curious. Sometimes, children hesitate to ask questions because they are shy, or they want to appear confident and knowledgeable in the eyes of others. Help them understand that asking questions can make them even more confident and knowledgeable because questions are the key to learning. Role-play situations in which children need to ask questions; for example, if they are lost, or they need help understanding a task they've been given, or they don't know the rules of a game.

Compliments

When others notice our efforts or respond to us positively, we can't help but feel special. Talk about compliments—what they are and why they leave others with a good feeling inside. Encourage children to offer a sincere compliment to someone else, and then to practice responding positively to a compliment that they've been given. Throughout the day, make a point of offering children encouragement: "I appreciate how you don't give up when you work on something challenging," or "I like the colors you chose for your drawing because they're so bright and cheery."

"I'm Sorry"

Young children are still in the process of learning to take responsibility for their words and actions. They often need encouragement when it comes to acknowledging a mistake or apologizing for something they've done. Talk about how two little words, "I'm sorry," can be so important when communicating with others. Point out that apologizing helps the other person feel better; sometimes, saying sorry can stop an argument in its tracks or prevent it from getting worse. Have children practice different ways to apologize. They can say "I'm sorry," or "I didn't mean what I said," or "Can you please forgive me?" Sometimes, people who have been fighting make peace by shaking hands or giving each other a hug. Talk about why these actions can help.

Words for Getting Help

Getting Help When Needed

Help children understand that there are times when we may need to use our voice, our words, and our body language to tell others "no." Children who practice saying the word "no" or who role-play taking action are more likely to stand up for themselves if they do face a situation in which they need help from a grown-up. Give each child a chance to act out asking for help in an emergency or in an uncomfortable situation.

> **Note:** If you suspect that a child is being abused, contact your local Social Service Department, Child Welfare Department, Police Department, or District Attorney's Office. If you teach in a public or private school setting, consult first with your school principal or director to learn the established course of action.

What Children Can Do If There Is Fighting at Home

- Think of a safe place to go when the fighting starts. Make a plan to get to that safe place quickly.

- In that safe place, you can draw, read, or play quietly.

- If you don't feel safe, you can use the telephone to call 911. The person who answers will ask you how they can help. You can tell the person your name and address, and say that there is a fight going on in your home.

- Find a grown-up you trust and talk to that person about the fighting. This person can be an aunt or uncle, a grandparent, a teacher, a neighbor you know well, a teacher, a caregiver, or a leader at your place of worship. You might say, "There is a lot of yelling and fighting in my home. I'm scared. Can you help?"

What Adults Can Do If There Is Fighting at Home

- Call 911.

- Call a local shelter or a domestic abuse hotline.

- Talk with someone who can help: a family counselor, a social worker, a therapist, or a member of the clergy. Your child's school counselor may also be a resource for you. If cost is an issue, it is possible to find low-cost or free services. Keep looking until you find a person or an organization that meets your needs.

- Stay with friends or relatives while you're getting the help you need.

Other Resources for Children

Feelings by Aliki, and *Manners* by Aliki (New York: Mulberry Books, 1986 and 1997 respectively). These two books use simple words and sweet illustrations to help children understand ways to talk about their feelings and treat others with consideration.

Hands Are Not for Hitting by Martine Agassi (Minneapolis: Free Spirit Publishing, 2000). The two main themes of this book are: violence is never okay, and every child is capable of positive, loving actions. Use this book as a companion to *Words Are Not for Hurting* to encourage kindness and respect. A board book for toddlers and preschool-age children is also available.

How to Be a Friend by Laurie Krasny Brown and Marc Brown (Boston: Little, Brown & Company, 1998). This guide to making and keeping friends helps children understand that being a friend means acting like one. Readers are encouraged to use words in kind ways, such as inviting someone to play, standing up for a friend when necessary, cooperating, giving compliments, being honest, and keeping their word.

How to Lose All Your Friends by Nancy L. Carlson (New York: Puffin, 1997). In this tongue-in-cheek "self-help" book, the author/illustrator offers tips on how to make all your friends stop liking you. She covers grouchiness, tattling, whining, and other not-so-friendly behaviors that put other people at a distance.

Roses Are Pink, Your Feet Really Stink by Diane de Groat (New York, Mulberry Books, 1996). With gentle humor, the author/illustrator of this picture book tells the story of Gilbert, who gets back at two classmates by writing them rude Valentines and pretending that they aren't from him. He learns that when his words hurt others, he feels hurt himself. His regret leads to a creative apology.

Simple Signs and *More Simple Signs* by Cindy Wheeler (New York: Puffin, 1997, and New York: Viking Children's Books, 1998). These fun and interactive books teach American Sign Language for many words that are familiar to young children. The text includes clear pictures with hints for how to make each sign.

We Can Get Along and *A Leader's Guide to We Can Get Along* by Lauren Murphy Payne and Claudia Rohling (Minneapolis: Free Spirit Publishing, 1997). The children's book teaches essential values such as kindness, responsibility, caring, and acceptance. The leader's guide includes reproducible masters such as "25 Healthy Ways to Express Anger" and "20 Things to Do Instead of Hurting Someone Back."

About the Author and Illustrator

Elizabeth Verdick is also the author of *Teeth Are Not for Biting* and *Words Are Not for Hurting* board books for toddlers. She is the coauthor (with Marjorie Lisovskis) of *How to Take the Grrrr Out of Anger* and has coauthored several books with Trevor Romain, including *Stress Can Really Get on Your Nerves!* and *True or False? Tests Stink!* She is the coauthor (with Pamela Espeland) of *Making Every Day Count.* Elizabeth has edited more than 30 books for children, teens, and adults, and writes a weekly parenting column called "Family Focus" for a central Minnesota newspaper. She lives with her husband and their two children near St. Paul, Minnesota.

Marieka Heinlen is also the illustrator of the *Teeth Are Not for Biting* and *Words Are Not for Hurting* board books, as well as the award-winning *Hands Are Not for Hitting* books for toddlers and preschoolers. As a Creative Director she designs and illustrates books and other materials for children, teens, parents, and teachers. She lives in St. Paul, Minnesota.

Other Great Books from Free Spirit

Words Are Not for Hurting
Board Book
by Elizabeth Verdick,
illustrated by Marieka Heinlen
Children are known for speaking their minds. We can't expect them to watch every word, but we can help them to understand that their words affect other people. For baby–preschool.
$7.95; 24 pp.; board book; color illus.; 7" x 7"

Teeth Are Not for Biting
Board Book
by Elizabeth Verdick,
illustrated by Marieka Heinlen
Almost all young children will bite someone. This book helps prevent biting and teaches positive alternatives. Includes helpful tips for parents and caregivers. For baby–preschool.
$7.95; 24 pp.; board book; color illus.; 7" x 7"

Hands Are Not for Hitting
Board Book
by Martine Agassi, Ph.D.,
illustrated by Marieka Heinlen
Created in response to requests from parents, preschool teachers, and childcare providers, the *Hands Are Not for Hitting* board book is perfect for little hands—because it's never too early to learn that violence is never okay, hands can do many good things, and every child is capable of positive, loving actions. Short, simple, colorful, and durable, this little book belongs everywhere young children are. For baby–preschool.
$7.95; 24 pp.; board book; color illus.; 7" x 7"

Feet Are Not for Kicking
Board Book
by Elizabeth Verdick,
illustrated by Marieka Heinlen
Feet are for walking, standing, leaping, and landing. They're for kicking balls or leaves—but not people! In simple words and charming full-color illustrations, this book helps little ones learn to use their feet for fun, not in anger or frustration. It also includes tips for parents and caregivers on how to help toddlers be sweet with their feet. For baby–preschool.
$7.95; 24 pp.; board book; color illus.; 7" x 7"

Hands Are Not for Hitting
by Martine Agassi, Ph.D.,
illustrated by Marieka Heinlen
In this gentle, encouraging book, psychologist Martine Agassi helps young children understand that they are capable of positive, loving actions. Simple words and warm, full-color illustrations reinforce the underlying concepts: that violence is never okay, and kids can learn to manage their anger. Made to be read aloud, it also includes a special section for adults, with ideas for things to talk about and activities to do together. For ages 4–7.
$11.95; 40 pp.; softcover; color illus.; 9" x 9"

To place an order or to request a free catalog of SELF-HELP FOR KIDS®
and SELF-HELP FOR TEENS® materials, please write, call, email, or visit our Web site:

Free Spirit Publishing Inc.
217 Fifth Avenue North • Suite 200 • Minneapolis, MN 55401-1299
toll-free 800.735.7323 • local 612.338.2068 • fax 612.337.5050
help4kids@freespirit.com • www.freespirit.com